This book is dedicated to my twin daughters who teach me something new every day. Love you my little Jinkers.

CAN WE PLAY WITH YOUR DOG?

Written by Dave Kitt. Illustrated by XhenXhen.

Let's go to the park
and play with dogs.

OK, but remember we must always ask if the dogs can play.

Can we play with your dog?

Sorry but he is
not feeling very
well.

Can we play with your dog?

Sorry but she is very big and might knock you over.

Can we play with your dog?

Sorry but he is a puppy and gets too excited.

Can we play with your dog?

Sorry but he is too old & tired to play.

Can we play with your dog?

Sorry but
she is afraid
of other
people.

Can we play with this dog?

Can we play with your dog?

Sorry but he is working right now.

Can we play with your dog?

Sorry but he is eating and does not like to share.

Can we play with your dogs?

Yes you can.
They love to
play with kids.

Do you know why I can't play with you?